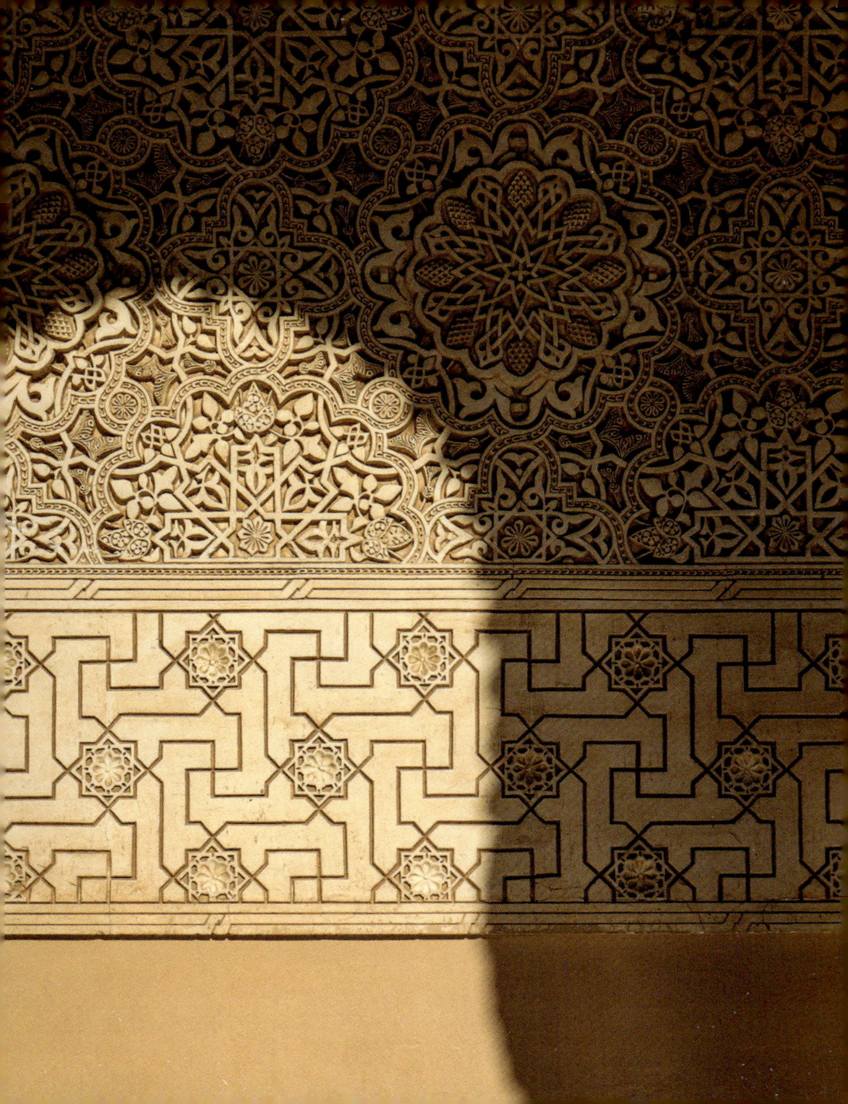

Nasrid Palaces

Mexuar
Comares
Leones

Triangle·Books

MEXUAR
THE MEXUAR

1 Court of Machuca
2 Hall of the Mexuar
3 Oratory
4 Gilded Room
5 Court of the Gilded Room

PALACIO DE COMARES
COMARES PALACE

6 Comares Façade
7 Court of the Myrtles
8 Hall of the Boat
9 Throne Room
10 Comares Tower
11 North Portico
12 South Portico
13 Comares Baths

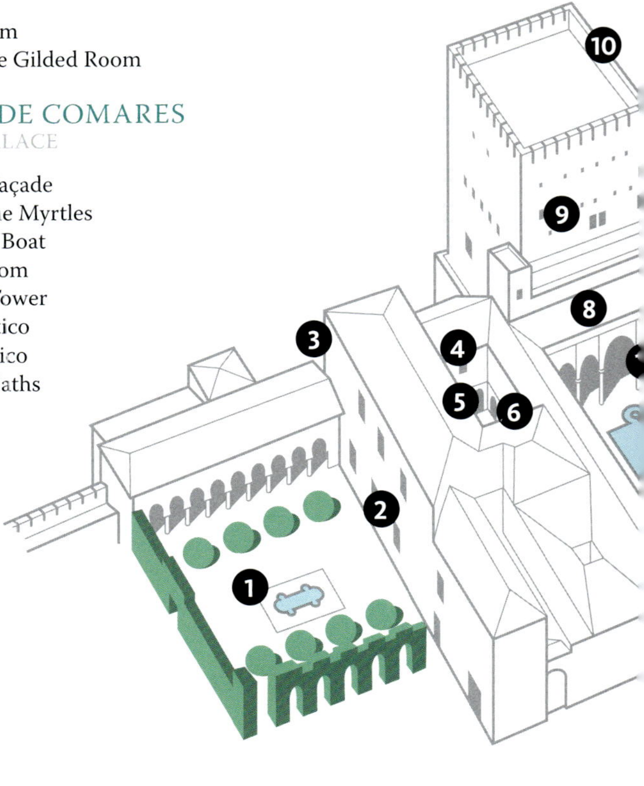

PALACIO DE LOS LEONES

PALACE OF THE LIONS

14 Hall of the Muqarnas
15 Court of the Lions
16 Hall of the Abencerrajes
17 Court of the Harem
18 Hall of the Kings
19 Hall of the Two Sisters
20 Hall of the Ajimeces
21 Lindaraja Balcony
22 Court of Lindaraja

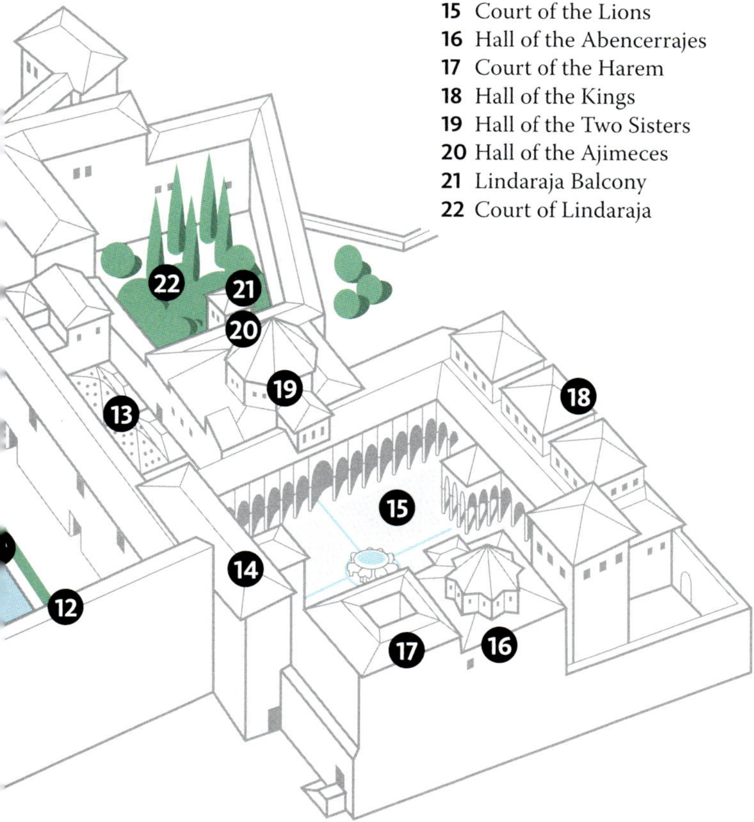

The Alhambra is a masterpiece of universal art on every scale. It appears majestic when viewed from afar, from the San Nicolás vantage point, facing the peaks of the Sierra Nevada, while also being dazzling up close, where we can relish in the delicacy of the filigrees that adorn its walls. Among the intricate set of fortresses, buildings and gardens that comprise them, the Nasrid Palaces (Palacios Nazaríes) stand out as the true heart of the citadel. Built in the 14th century, they were home to the sovereigns of the Nasrid dynasty. This is where their court worked, and also where they impressed their guests, who were left in awe by the contrast of the austerity of the exterior and the ostentation of the chambers and courtyards, which have survived to the present day somewhat transformed, yet enviably well preserved.

THE MEXUAR

The Mexuar was likely the palace's primitive throne room, before becoming the place where the Nasrid court gathered and the Sultan dispensed justice. Following the conquest of Granada in 1492, the Catholic Monarchs turned it into a chapel and ordered an additional floor to be built, thus covering the skylight that previously illuminated the hall. Despite these changes, the decoration of the Mexuar continues to convey the sense of power for which it was originally intended.

▲ The Mexuar owes its name to the Arabic word *maswar*, which designates the place where the Sultan's counsel gathered. The hall's flooring, which combines baked clay tiles and tiles adorned with heraldic symbols, was made after the Muslim rule.

▸ In the original layout of the Mexuar, the hall's four columns held a central lantern to illuminate the space. The renovations conducted in the 16th century replaced the Nasrid lantern with a splendid, coffered ceiling crafted in wood.

▲ Detail of the tiled panel of the hall of the Mexuar, which combines the Nasrid technique with symbols of Greco-Roman origin, in this case the pillars of Hercules.

▶ The Oratory of the Mexuar disrupts the alignment of the adjacent chambers to face Mecca and provides magnificent views of the Albaicín district.

▲ The side door of the Court of the Gilded Room (Cuarto Dorado), which leads into the hall of the Mexuar.

▶ The portico's central arch which leads into the Gilded Room.

▲ The delicate plasterwork shines on the arches, capitals and walls of the courtyard.

▸ The refined workmanship of the plasterwork is apparent in this close-up of one of the capitals of the portico in the Gilded Room.

COMARES PALACE

The extraordinary decoration on the façade of Comares Palace (Palacio de Comares), to the south of the Court of the Gilded Room, which was inaugurated in 1370 by Sultan Muhammad V, foreshadows the sumptuosity of Comares Palace, the area in which court representation duties were carried out. Among the set of chambers surrounding the Court of the Myrtles (Patio de los Arrayanes), which features a pond upon which the adjacent buildings cast their reflection, the Throne Room stands out as the largest room in the fortress and the place where the Sultan received foreign emissaries.

▲ An example of the combination of geometric and botanic designs that characterise the decoration of the façade of Comares Palace.

◂ Detail of the tiled panel on the façade of Comares Palace.

The chambers of Comares Palace are arranged around the Court of the Myrtles, with two porticoed façades on the shorter sides which led into the representation rooms, and two longer façades that concealed private chambers. At the far end stands the Comares Tower (Torre de Comares), the tallest structure of the Alhambra.

▲ The *alhanías* (*alhaníyyas*), small bedrooms that flanked the porticoes of the Court of the Myrtles, feature delicate examples of tiled panels (above), as well as muqarnas and plasterwork.

▸ The south-facing façade of the Court of the Myrtles comprises a ground floor and two upper floors. The top floor recreates the same arrangement as the ground floor: a seven-arch portico, but here the central arch is lintelled. The structure that stood behind the façade was demolished when the palace of Charles V was built. In the following pages, the north-facing façade is seen reflected in the pond.

▲ Detail of polychromatic muqarnas that adorn the vaults of the *alhanías*, small bedrooms that open up at the sides of the porticoes.

► In the porticoes of the Court of Myrtles, the overlaying of the plasterwork on the tiled panels creates an intriguing architectural effect.

▲ The immense ceiling of the Throne Room, comprised of geometrically shaped wooden pieces, draws inspiration from the seven heavens of the Quran, which culminate in the eighth, where Allah resides.

▶ View of the arches of different morphology that run across the Hall of the Boat (Sala de la Barca) and open onto the Court of the Myrtles.

Details of the ornamentation of two of the nine chambers within the thick walls of the Throne Room, with the latticework that provides subtle side lighting to the chamber.

Two of the baths in Comares, in which the vault with star-shaped skylights stands out.

Over the Hall of the Beds (Sala de las Camas) of the Bath of Comares are the chambers on the upper floor, lit by a lantern formed of 16 arched bays that open to the four cardinal points.

PALACE OF THE LIONS

A discreet arch to one end of the Court of the Myrtles leads to the Palace of the Lions (Palacio de los Leones), a private area where the Sultan and his wives could live with almost no contact with the world outside. In each of the main chambers, channels begin which ultimately converge in the famous Fountain of the Lions (Fuente de los Leones), echoing the four rivers of Paradise as described in the Quran. Here, the harmony between architecture, ornamentation and water reaches its pinnacle.

◂ The column forest in the galleries of the courtyard is crowned with capitals of very varied shapes.

▴ Detail of one of the twelve famous marble lions that support the fountain in the courtyard.

“Water and marble seem to be one, without letting us know which of them is flowing.” This excerpt pertains to the twelve verses of the Granadan poet Ibn Zamrak (1333-1393) engraved on the fountain to celebrate the beauty of the space. Both the basin and the twelve lions are made in white marble sourced from the nearby Macael quarries, in the province of Almería.

Above, the Hall of the Kings (Sala de los Reyes), a long nave onto which three bedrooms open. To the left, the arches of one of the entrances to the hall.

▸▸ On the following pages, the central dome of the Hall of the Kings, depicting the first ten monarchs of the Nasrid dynasty which lends its name to the hall.

Lit by the sun that pours in through the upper windows, the refined muqarnas that adorn the domes in the bedrooms of the Hall of the Kings seem to shine with a light of their own.

The spectacular muqarnas dome in the Hall of the Abencerrajes (Sala de los Abencerrajes) provides a brilliant transition from the square plan of the room to the star-shaped roof.

◂ View from the Hall of the Two Sisters (Sala de Dos Hermanas), with the channel that connects to the Fountain of the Lions.

▴ The octagonal muqarnas dome, standing on a star-shaped base, is the most prominent feature of the space.

The channel that flows from the Hall of the Two Sisters to the Fountain of the Lions runs under arches and vaults adorned with highly delicate ornamental motifs.

The central arch in the Court of the Harem, the entrance to the innermost area of the building, where the Sultan and his family lived out of sight of officials and courtiers.

The latticework added to the privacy of the royal chambers. Magnificent plaster inscriptions decorate the upper and lower bands of the window arches.

▲ The architecture surrounding the Court of the Lindaraja (Patio de la Lindaraja), presided over by an observation point of the same name, resembles a cloister and dates back to the Christian era, although the landscaping may have been similar during the Muslim period.

▶ Adjacent to the Hall of the Two Sisters, the observation point of Daraxa or Lindaraja Balcony afforded the Sultan a view over the court of the same name along with the whole of Granada. The panoramic view over the city was blocked by the construction of the palace of Charles V in 1526.

Sant Lluís, Menorca
triangle@triangle.cat
www.triangle.cat

Text
© Ricard Regàs

Photography
© Pere Vivas
Laia Moreno, p. 8, 41, 60, 61, 62
Hans Hansen, p. 10, 17, 18, 26, 52
Ricard Pla, p. 48

Translation
Bcn Babel. Ana Pedrero

Design
David Martínez

Printed by
Agpograf
Printed in Spain, 4-2024

Registration number Me 119-2024

ISBN 978-84-1012-718-0

Triangle·Books